TICKET TO THE

FIFA
WORLD CUP

MARTIN GITLIN

ADMIT ONE

THE BIG GAME

YOUR FRONT ROW SEAT

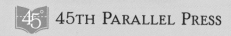

45TH PARALLEL PRESS

Published in the United States of America by Cherry Lake Publishing Group
Ann Arbor, Michigan
www.cherrylakepublishing.com

Reading Adviser: Beth Walker Gambro, MS Ed., Reading Consultant, Yorkville, IL
Book Designer: Jen Wahi

Photo Credits: Cover: © Mikolaj Barbanell/Shutterstock; page 5: © A.RICARDO/Shutterstock; page 7: © Asatur Yesayants/Shutterstock; page 9: © Celso Pupo/Shutterstock; page 11: © Fabio Diena/Dreamstime.com; page 17: © Jose Breton- Pics Action/Shutterstock; page 21: © Alizada Studios/Shutterstock; page 22: © Andre Ricardo/Dreamstime. com; page 25: © cristiano barni/Shutterstock; page 27: © Vitalii Kliuiev/Dreamstime.com; page 28 (top): © Zhukovsky/ Dreamstime.com; page 28 (bottom): © Zhukovsky/Dreamstime.com

Copyright © 2023 by Cherry Lake Publishing Group

All rights reserved. No part of this book may be reproduced or utilized in any form or by any means without written permission from the publisher.

45th Parallel Press is an imprint of Cherry Lake Publishing Group.

Library of Congress Cataloging-in-Publication Data

Names: Gitlin, Martin, author.
Title: Ticket to the FIFA World Cup / Martin Gitlin.
Description: Ann Arbor, Michigan : Cherry Lake Publishing, [2023] | Series: The big game | Audience: Grades 4-6 | Summary: "Who has won the FIFA World Cup? How did they make it to the final game? Written as high interest with struggling readers in mind, this series includes considerate vocabulary, engaging content and fascinating facts, clear text and formatting, and compelling photos. Educational sidebars include extra fun facts and information about each game. Include table of contents, glossary, index, and author biography"-- Provided by publisher.
Identifiers: LCCN 2022039700 | ISBN 9781668919521 (hardcover) | ISBN 9781668920541 (paperback) | ISBN 9781668923207 (pdf) | ISBN 9781668921876 (ebook)
Subjects: LCSH: World Cup (Soccer)--Juvenile literature. | Soccer--History--Juvenile literature. | Soccer--Miscellanea--Juvenile literature.
Classification: LCC GV943.49 .G48 2023 | DDC 796.334/668--dc23/eng/20220901
LC record available at https://lccn.loc.gov/2022039700

Cherry Lake Publishing would like to acknowledge the work of the Partnership for 21st Century Learning, a network of Battelle for Kids. Please visit http://www.battelleforkids.org/networks/p21

Printed in the United States of America
Corporate Graphics

Table of Contents

Introduction

It is called soccer in the United States. It is called football in most countries. But one thing is certain. It is the most popular sport in the world.

Soccer takes a back seat in the United States. More fans follow American football. Or they prefer baseball. Basketball also gets much attention.

But soccer has grown in the United States. Millions of kids play it. Millions more watch it in person and on TV.

Interest rises every 4 years. That is when the World Cup is played. Some think it is the biggest sporting event on Earth.

There is a men's World Cup. There is a women's World Cup. Both are held every 4 years. But each is played in different years.

Kylian Mbappé kisses the FIFA World Cup trophy after France's win in 2018.

Teams from 32 countries compete. The winners move on. They keep playing until only 1 team is left. That is the champion.

Soccer is a low-scoring sport. Often only 1 goal is scored in a match.

Most goals come when the ball is kicked into the net. Sometimes they are scored on headers. That is when a ball bounces off a player's head into the net.

Goalkeepers stand in front of the net. They try to stop balls from going in the net.

Some countries are known for their strong teams. Men's teams from South America have won many World Cups. So have those from Europe.

The U.S. men's team still hadn't reached the World Cup finals as of 2018. That match decides the World Cup title.

The women's World Cup is a different story. The U.S. team has won 4 of the 8 events since 1991.

Dejan Lovren of Croatia hits the ball with a header in a match against Argentina in 2018.

History of the Men's Cup

The men's World Cup began in 1930. But international soccer was around before then. International events are where different countries compete.

The first men's event was the Sir Thomas Lipton Trophy. That was in 1909.

The Summer Olympics also had soccer. But the players did not get paid to play.

By 1928 the best players were being paid. So FIFA stepped in. That is the International Federation of Association Football. It runs international soccer. FIFA began to plan the World Cup.

The first one was 2 years later. It was held in Uruguay in South America. The first event had 13 teams.

Edinson Cavani plays for Uruguay during a 2014 World Cup game against England.

Uruguay won the first World Cup. The United States finished third. No U.S. team placed that high again through 2018.

The Uruguay team liked winning the Cup for its home fans. So did Italy in 1934. That European country hosted the event. And Italy thrilled its fans by taking the crown.

Many feel that team had the best Italian player ever. His name was Guiseppe Meazza. He was the star of the 1934 World Cup winners. He also led Italy to the 1938 title. He scored an amazing 33 goals in international events.

In 1942, the event did not take place. World War II was raging. Battles were fought with guns rather than soccer balls.

The war was over by 1946. But Europe and much of Asia had been destroyed. Nations worked to recover from the war. They had no time for soccer.

The World Cup came back in 1950. And it returned with its original champion. The event was held in Brazil. And that country made the finals. But Uruguay beat Brazil for the cup.

Uruguay was a much smaller country than Brazil. It had far fewer people. But Uruguay was a soccer power. Many were not surprised that they beat Brazil.

Paolo Maldini is known as one of the greatest Italian soccer players of all time.

Among those hurt by the Brazil loss was Pelé. He was perhaps the greatest soccer player ever. Pelé remains a legend.

Pelé was just 9 years old in 1950. But he loved soccer. He recalled his father crying after Brazil lost. He told his dad he would help his country win a World Cup.

That is just what he did. Pelé helped Brazil to World Cup victories in 1958, 1962, and 1970.

Pelé first played in the Cup at age 17. He wasted no time making an impact. He scored 3 goals in a semifinals win over France. The semifinals are the games that determine who will play in the finals. Then he scored 2 in a finals defeat of Sweden.

The superstar made Brazil a soccer power. He scored 12 goals in 14 World Cup matches.

Pelé's last World Cup was in 1970. His decision to stop playing gave other countries a better chance to win. Germany won the Cup in 1974 and 1990. Argentina took it in 1978 and 1986. Those 2 teams had amazing players.

Many felt the Uruguay win in 1950 was an upset. This is when a team you thought would win loses.

Most believed Uruguay was a huge underdog. That means it was expected to lose.

Brazil was supposed to win. And they were winning.

But Uruguay star Juan Alberto Schiaffino changed that. His goal tied the match at 1–1. Then teammate Alcides Ghiggia scored to win it.

WAY BACK WHEN

Germany and Argentina took turns beating each other. Argentina defeated Germany in the 1986 finals. Germany got revenge in the 1990 finals.

Argentina star Diego Maradona was amazing in 1986. He scored 5 goals and had 5 assists. An assist is a pass that leads to a goal.

Maradona played hero in the finals. He made the winning assist to break a 2–2 tie. That gave Argentina the World Cup title.

The men's World Cup kept growing. More countries joined the event. It rose from 16 to 24 in 1982. And it grew to 32 teams in 1998.

That meant more stars on the biggest stage. Among them was Ronaldo Nazário. He led Brazil to the title in 2002. He finished his World Cup career with 15 goals. Only 1 German player, Miroslav Klose, has more at 16 goals.

Teams in Europe have since ruled soccer. The only one to make the finals twice was France.

All but one had won the Cup before. The only exception was Spain. That country snagged its first crown in 2010.

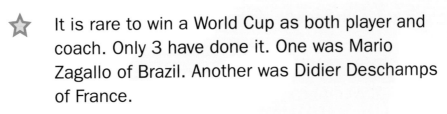

★ It is rare to win a World Cup as both player and coach. Only 3 have done it. One was Mario Zagallo of Brazil. Another was Didier Deschamps of France.

★ The third was the best player of all. His name was Franz Beckenbauer. He helped Germany win the World Cup in 1974. He is perhaps the greatest German player ever.

★ Beckenbauer was not done leading Germany to victory. He became its head coach. And he guided it to another title in 1990. Many believe Beckenbauer is among the best players in soccer history.

LEGENDS OF THE SPORT

History of the Women's Cup

A women's soccer event was held in Italy in 1970. It was not the World Cup. But it drew many fans. An idea was born.

In 1988, FIFA invited women to play. That was in China. That was also a success.

That success led to the Women's World Cup. It was first held in 1991. And the U.S. women did what its men never did. They won the title. They claimed it with a 2–1 defeat of Norway.

The United States was not done dominating. It won the Women's World Cup again in 1999. It lost to Japan in the 2011 finals. Then it took first place in 2015 and 2019.

Megan Rapinoe helped the U.S. women's team win the FIFA Women's World Cup in 2019.

Many stars from those teams gained fame. Among them was Mia Hamm. She played in 4 World Cups. She helped the United States win in 1991 and 1999.

Hamm scored 8 goals in those matches. And she added 3 assists. Many think she is the best women's soccer player ever.

Others believe the greatest was Marta. Her Brazil team did not win a World Cup through 2019. But she scored more Cup goals than any other woman. Marta sent 15 shots into the net.

Marta won FIFA Player of the Year 6 times. She took the honor every year from 2006 to 2010, and again in 2013.

Only 1 country other than the United States has won more than 1 Cup. Germany snagged the title in 2003 and 2007.

★ The Japanese women's team did something special in 2011. It won the World Cup.

★ Japan was the first Asian team to take the title.

★ No men's or women's team from that continent had ever done it. No Asian men's team has even reached the finals.

!A BIT OF TRIVIA

Great Matches and Moments

The year was 1970. The place was Mexico City. The event was a men's World Cup semifinal. West Germany battled Italy for a spot in the finals. At the time, Germany was split into two countries. They were West Germany and East Germany.

Some feel it was the greatest Cup match ever. It got very exciting.

Italy had a 2–1 lead. It appeared Italy would take home the crown. Time was running out.

West German fans finally got a chance to cheer. That was when Karl-Heinz Schnellinger scored. The goal tied the match.

Antonio Rüdiger is a present-day German soccer player who plays for the Germany national team. There is no longer a West Germany team.

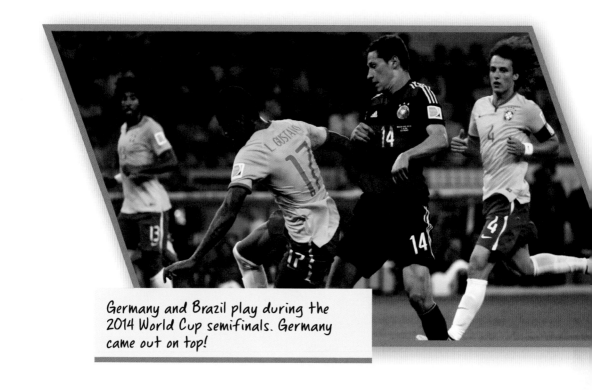

Germany and Brazil play during the 2014 World Cup semifinals. Germany came out on top!

The match went into extra time. That is when regular time ends in a tie. Gerd Müller scored for West Germany. Tarcisio Burgnich and Gigi Riva then scored for Italy.

West Germany was behind again. But it refused to give up. Müller sent a header past the Italian goalkeeper. That tied the match.

Most World Cup matches are low-scoring and close. But not the 2014 men's battle between Germany and Brazil.

The match was in Brazil. Its team had not lost at home in 39 years. But Brazil did not just fall to Germany. It was smashed.

Germany won the match 7–1. It then beat Argentina for its third World Cup crown.

AMAZING MOMENT

One more goal from either side would win it. And that was scored by Italy's Gianni Rivera. He kicked the ball into the net. It was finally over.

But Italy could not keep up its magic. Pelé and Brazil were too strong. Brazil beat Italy in the finals to win the Cup.

Brazilian Alex Sandro plays for the Brazil national soccer team. Brazil has won the World Cup 5 times.

Exciting Endings

Sometimes a goal ends the World Cup. That is always a thrilling moment. It happened in 2010.

That game was the final between Spain and the Netherlands. The Netherlands had lost finals in 1974 and 1978.

Defense ruled the match. Neither team could score. The battle went into extra time. Spain had control of the ball. Its players were surrounded by defenders.

The ball landed at the feet of Spain's Andrés Iniesta. He kicked the ball with his right foot. It headed toward the left corner of the net.

Netherlands goalkeeper Maarten Stekelenburg dove for the ball. But he missed. It landed in the net. Spain had won the match and the Cup.

Dutch player Memphis Depay (known as Memphis) plays for the Netherlands national team. The Dutch have played in the most World Cup finals without winning.

U.S. player Alex Morgan takes the ball down the field in a match against Mexico before the 2019 Women's World Cup.

Tobin Heath, forward on the U.S. Women's National team, was voted the 2016 U.S. Soccer Athlete of the Year.

Exciting endings have not been limited to men's soccer. The U.S. women's team won an exciting game in 1999.

It was played before a huge crowd. More than 90,000 fans packed the Rose Bowl in Los Angeles. They were in for a treat.

The U.S. team was playing China for the title. U.S. player Brandi Chastain led her team to victory. She booted a penalty kick into the net. That is a shot that the other team is not allowed to defend.

Chastain sent the ball past the diving goalkeeper. It gave the U.S. women their second World Cup crown.

Activity

Practice kicking a soccer ball near your home. Join a soccer team for kids your age. Play with friends or family members. Learn about the positions on a soccer team. Then decide which you would like to play.

Learn More

BOOKS

Bader, Bonnie. *What Is the World Cup?* New York: Penguin Workshop, 2018.

Nhin, Kobe, and Mary Nhin. *How to Win the World Cup in Pajamas: Mental Toughness for Kids*. Oklahoma City, OK: Grow Grit Press, 2019.

Walters, Meg. *World Cup Women: Megan, Alex, and the Team USA Soccer Champs*. New York: Sky Pony, 2019.

WEBSITES

Britannica Kids: World Cup: https://kids.britannica.com/kids/article/World-Cup/390872

Kiddle: FIFA Facts for Kids: https://kids.kiddle.co/FIFA

Sports Illustrated Kids: Soccer: https://www.sikids.com/tag/soccer

Glossary

assists (uh-SISTS) passes that lead to a goal

extra time (EK-struh TYM) playing time added to a tie game

FIFA (FYE-fuh) group that runs international soccer

finals (FYE-nuhls) match that determines the World Cup champion

goal (GOHL) ball kicked or headed into the net to score a point

goalkeeper (GOHL-kee-puhr) player who tries to stop shots from going into the net

headers (HEH-duhrs) shots that bounce off a player's head

international (in-tuhr-NAH-shuh-nuhl) countries and places around the world

penalty kick (PEH-nuhl-tee kik) undefended shot awarded after a penalty by the other team

semifinals (seh-mee-FYE-nuhls) matches that determine which teams meet in the finals

underdog (UHN-duhr-dawg) player or team given little chance to win

upset (UHP-set) unexpected win by a team

Index

About the Author

Marty Gitlin is a sports book author based in Cleveland. He won more than 45 awards as a newspaper sportswriter from 1991 to 2002. Included was a first-place award from the Associated Press for his coverage of the 1995 World Series. He has had more than 200 books published since 2006. Most of them were written for students.